# THE FLAWSOME PHOENIX

## POEMS TO CONNECT YOUR HEART TO MINE AND THEN CALL IT HOME.

## SOURISHREE GHOSH

ISBN 979-888555567-8

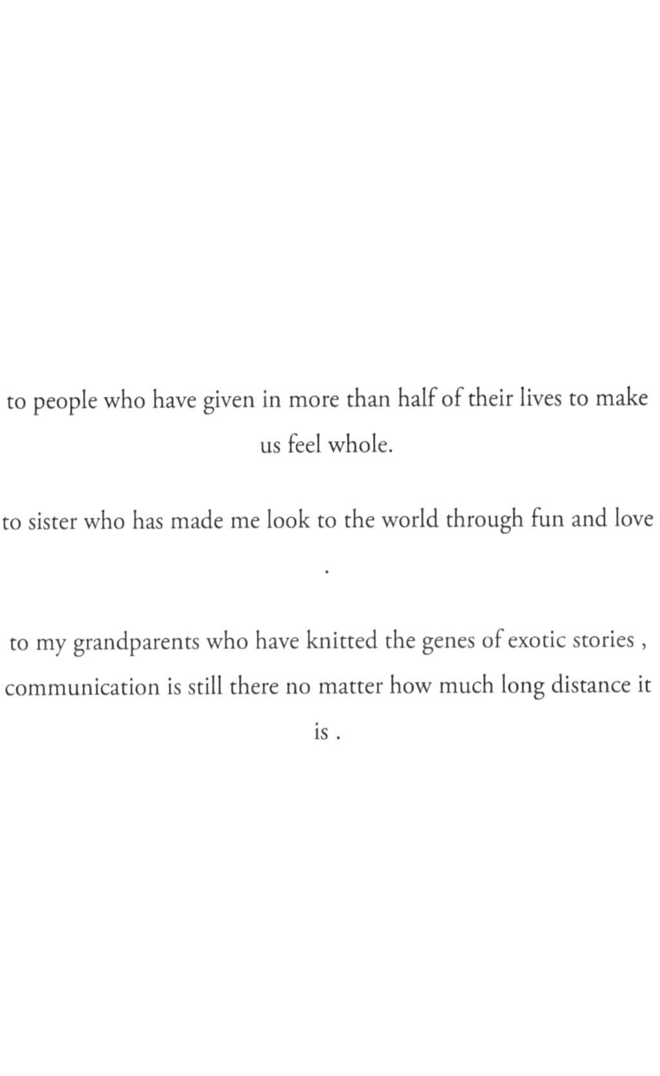

to people who have given in more than half of their lives to make us feel whole.

to sister who has made me look to the world through fun and love

.

to my grandparents who have knitted the genes of exotic stories , communication is still there no matter how much long distance it is .

# Contents

# Foreword

This is a work of poems moulded by an artist . if you read them, you can go back to them again in your life if needed . it holds different perspectives from broken love to self-love . it is a take on different themes like love , nature , sarcastic , tragedy , opinions and the list is unending . this book contains intricately stitiched poems woven into your soul and your everyday life as a whole . the next series is on the way .

# Preface

this is my first poetry collection about experiences and observations which i thought the best way to give voice is writing a book . today's world is moving faster than expected and i thought that readers would find this book precise as well as amazing .

# Acknowledgements

i would like to acknowledge the efforts of my parents who have been guiding me throughout and encouraging me to take brave decisons and experiment with life . Notion Press has provided this great opportunity of dreams coming true of a writer transforming into an author . i would also remain grateful to my taechers who have always tried to find out the best in me .

# Prologue

thanks for deciding to purchaing this book and i hope you will not regret it. let us move forward as the world is . let us dive into this world to recognize the best version of you ! this is my first collection of poetry as an author .

# 1. WRITERS ARE GHOSTS

we are ghosts living in your moments you take for granted,
you can't time us on clock because words are infinite .
we choke you wrapping in the blanket of paper ,
and you lay your heart open as you tell problems to a doctor .
your stories and experiences are buried in the safe coffin of pages ,
which people of all age read over ages , which are never enough old.
we are void enough to fill all your emptiness in your hearts ,
we are ghosts as important as your suitcases.

# 2. What a Calender holds?

like you hold a pearl in your palm ,
hold it to the Sun to shine brighter than the shadows which
run ,
a calendar holds time , hopes and exceptions ,
together in a bundled color of seasons full of reasons .
a calendar is like burning time with bearing logs of consistent-
hardwork,
a calendar as happy as those surprises on birthday nights ,
a calendar is not about holding dates but counting fights.
a calendar hangs like a pendulim on the walls too old to hold
memories .
the footnotes like that of an excerpt or a memoir,
juggling between needs and deeds ,;ife it is .
some dates too empty , some too overloaded ,
the calendar is our brand , a hat we are struggling to maintain
in dusty-frosty wind.

# 3. Journey and its Journal

The journey of life won't take us to the fleeting clouds and painted rainbows ,

we build all our values around spaces we confine ourselves called a home ,

some journeys are like promises made , fullfilled halfway or saved as a legacy ,

some journeys are too sweet or too bitter to start ,life is an adventure .

no journey has a sad or a happy endings , change is permanent and life must end,

journey is a bookshelf and we are librarians reading , finding and adopting .

journey has written a journal through all those lone sea-breakers and wind-seekers of the World .

and as attention seeking as faces without masks .

# 4. SHE

She is the one wandering around you , seeking and living just
like nay other human being ,
answer me then , what difference her stains makes that she is
confined ?
her path is full of cob-webs more man-made than natural .
she is another name for the God you worship everyday for
blessings .
she tries her best to mop away the allegations against her ,
bruised , overwhelmed by a tag of costly democracy .
her eyes are like burning sand crying water at the cost of her
future ,
her own happiness , her own individuality like oasis or mirage
in deserts.
her motherly smile , sisterly huge , fatherly earnings ,
brotherly discipline
are the sterotypes she broke , some call her 'unobeying ',some
empowered .
her mood is expected to be family , unrest and riotic , as she
jurys any family struggle ,
still she doesn't own the keys of her home and her phone .
she has to learn herself , as society has failed to recognise her
needs ,

she has to learn to be a bird to fly head held-high across the
sky ,
before she could mother her daughters learn to deny !

• 5 •

# 5. Money and honey

money is the medicine for those sick of poverty,

money is an addiction for the greedy .

money is a little painful ,not plain-ful difficult to handle an

uncaged bird ,

it may fly to you ,if wounded for sometime , or join the herd .

money is painful when comes to giving or money is

comforting when comes to taking ,

money is all that it takes for a living .

money is the weapon for all these mess ,

a political game too hard as an the pyschological examination

.

there nothing as beautiful and dangerous as money just like

the human heart ,

money is a game , some use it black without any shame ,

money is not a layman's game .

money is a lot like writing ,

# 6. whenever you feel lonely

whenever you feel lonely or too restless to acknowledge it ,
whenever your hands vibrate to write the first lines of poetry ,
calling it a draft , not liked by the world you may think ,
but don't let all your dreams of writing sink .
there to connect you with worldly feelings or might be a link.
whenever you feel lonely , think of the glory if you live through this ,
whenever you feel lonely , sit realxed , arms stretching out to the sky catching stars ,
and making constellations of love i loved and hold them crumbled like the first draft .

# 7. what others say and we think it may

we crossed fingers and toes whatever we could ,

or better to be cheap , what we should .

we are followed by other's instincts more than our own ,

the World is smething more than shown ,

like the conditions of loan .

we sat together listening to stories we didn't think of,

and told solutions from our perspective ,

when you crossed a black cat , neighbors would look at or
look upon you ,

and waiting there , you later stand in a queue .

# 8. Exam Ghazal

the pain is more heavy than a scary ride , not good for health

,

cramming head before exams , found somewhere around book shelves.

once you scartch your head ,once you look around and no definite answer to be found ,

you fear of losing marks as if parents and teachers were like sharks .

we look for hints in our environment , this year we couldn't in confinement,

in those shuffle and sounds , we lose marks in pounds .

so , what do you think , a terribly dark tale , should exams be banned forever?

no, then how can we write such amazing ghazals .

exams are like poems wanting to be vomited , remembered and all that pain needed to be felt,

and then with your over-burdened shelf you knelt .

# 9. I am a mess

everybody states that I'm a mess ,
i am always busy even during my recess ,
i call myself my feelings a bit of excess ,
people call me a bundle of excuses .
i am a mess that none can clear ,
a nerve examination everyone fears ,
no one calls me their dear ,
still everybody is so near .
i am a mess you can never comprehend ,
the stormy road none can apprehend .
neither do i borrow nor i lend ,
praying for your well being is all i can send ,
flirting is all love can blend .
i am a mess curled up like disorted threads ,
not to stitch into a sweater , a warm and comfortable poem
this winter .
i am in a mess like fingers strangled in a fight ,
i am a kite , still waiting for my flight .

# 10. Listen

listen child , don't open doors to strangers ,
as it can bring uncertain dangers ,
you won't be able to fight like Avengers .
listen child , don't believe your friends too much ,
you might land up in trouble such and such ,
never lose your parent's clutch .
listen child , don't fetch too far ,
or miles roaming from deserts to deserts , don't dare ,
or the criminals or the decievers won't care ,
and you won't even get a birthday share .
listen child , look if you have left anything behind from where
you come ,
or as you grow this into a habit , you might lose a handsome
sum .
listen child , don't edge for freedom ,
otherwise you may fall for flying boredom ,
and we call it a teenage syndrome .
Grow in size ,not in shame , don't always try to find who is to
blame ,
that question is lame , don't try to fit in such media game .
listen , don't forget people who helped ,need your help ,
don't look at future far more than what you look at the present
or learn from the past.

then , life won't be pleasant.

# 11. here we are again

here we are again ,

dancing in the form of constellation of shadows ,

like a prince and a princess in a happy castle ,

forgetting it is made up of sand ,

unsecured , vulnerable to the waters of the world,

would you still become the shore of my tears?

here we are again ,

holding hands up to the Sun ignoring the food burn ,

lying against myself , that's the greatest sin i have ever committed ,

the greatest myth i have made myself believe into ,

and here you are again , to hold me

# 12. The Musings Of The Soul

there are a thousand thoughts drumming in my head ,

you can see sweats like rivers flowing across all bends ,

you can smell my feelings of anxiety and stress ,

or weirdly happiest of all i can embrace .

there are thousands of twangling instruments playing in my mind ,

as if someone is partying late at night with the speaker unkind ,

there are thousands nights to live for or you can't choose from ,

before i take shelter in another womb .

the sky is full of kites flying , aiming high ,

with wings of perseverance for further life's road clearance .

the soul has a loud music ,for a writer , it is musings ,

we know our instruments ,but have no idea about the songs we can play .

# 13. stopping here

like mirrors when they broke show more or less of each piece of the room ,
i am waiting to be broken to look more real , seeking perspective.
if your eyes are like balzing diamonds , with every cut of hope ,
better you know exceptations can be as tricky-pricky as soap .
stop here , turn all around , stops understanding walking back and looking back ,
the present halted , the future blotted and the past pleasured , all you do is on your leisure.
poetry is as simple yet complicated like water , you may call it rain and it sounds like tears .
don't pickpocket me , i have other stories to tell when i reach home .
stop here , lick your own wounds first than you heal other lives .

# 14. into a new year

i walk alone silently as the virus spreads into a new year,
fearing what the next wave would be like ,
or feeling disgusted at how people flouted norms once vaccinated ,
too much tired to forward the same messages ,
or as crazy as making a meme of myself ,
or the loud music that pumped up my heart into sleep light mare .
this year smells new fresh like honey , pure ones ,unadultearted with events,
it tastes like an ice-cream in summer , a hot coffee in winter
not letting the mind be as pleasant as spring or autumn .
drinking the night and its stars on a Christmas night ,
through the wide window i look ,
through the deepness of the darkness , loops of celebration amid the hollow cold .
then , i remember a rhyme which i hymn like a prayer everyday i went to school,
learned it from friends , surroundings and experience ,
life is short ,as you think about it , days and nights will pass ,
like wind blowing past beruffled hairs , going crazy and phenomenal sea waves ,
life is too short for saves .

# 15. and the birds flew all at once

a million questions a baby bird asks her mother about flying ,
or better hsving suicidal thoughts to skip this stage ,
then her mother taught her about the terrifying cage.
but who knows its the start of the life ,
like a baby comes to life after crying ,
that's not the last cry though ,
similarly , the fly is not the last .
a million questions would be answered before the last flight ,
and life never seemed so light .
and the birds without thinking twice gave their flight ,
and maybe they are not lost or are trying to find themselves .
raise your voice not against yourself ,but against the world that ,
forces to become against your own self .

# 16. Nature

nature has always rested welcomes me as a guest ,

for a comfortable not necessarily a grand fest ,

i should lose all that i took for granted lest ,

passing through the Nature's test in search for an eternal hest ,

life is simple yet intricate as the bird's nest .

writing about nature is like getting an earthquake coming with its own pros .

grief is a remainder that good things are waiting for their turn ,

nature is the home to all humanity , no matter how build your cement kingdom.

nature is the silence artists can feel with an energetic drill ,

nature chooses the best , like a tailor picking the brightest chalk ,

flowing winds kisses the trees , rainwater kisses the trees ,

nature is all we need to feel loved ,

nature is a languague that true admirers understand .

# 17. the last few

the last few days of the absolutely reckless year with pitiless
rain ,
the last few hours until the new year's morn as the old days
vain .
the last few breaths taken will become a memory of how it felt
to be alive ,
the last few moments with a dying friend is how pain felt ,
counting the stars , and then puffing smoke through the
engine of life .
the new year sometimes seems lonelier as some people leave
this world ,
the new year seems hopeful as some are born the next year.
it is beautiful that seasons pass by ,holding hands with my art-
pie .
its cruel how the virus blurred like wearing the wrong
spectacle ,
with all the uncertainity the share market holds .
i am already broken by anonymous and ambiguous
conversations,
i am living for a direction,but don't know the map and its
stations ,
accidents are more impactful than the safe journeys through
life .